The Four Channels: A Businesswoman's Guide to Cracking Confidence

Margo C. McClimans

CONTENTS

ACKNOWLEDGEMENTS

To my sister and parents, thank you for the unconditional love; it has made all the difference in my life! I am grateful. I love you!

To my clients and fellow coaches, thank you for being willing to open yourselves to me. I learn and grow every time I have the privilege to work with you. This book is possible thanks to our experiences together.

Carla Picardi, my official unofficial coach, official role model and dear friend, thank you for opening my eyes to the wonderful world of possibilities!.

Lizzie (I'm excited to be friends forever!) Jarvis. Thank you for your always being there for me and reminding me to bring mindfulness into this book!

Gareth Robinson, thank you for your loving support.

Suzie Doscher, you inspire me and blazed the trail of self-publishing for us, thank you!

Teresa Hurcik, thank you for your endless dedication and hard work!

Friends not named here, I treasure each and every one of you. Thank you for being in my life.

And two people deserve special honor, who helped me cross that daunting "start" line on this book and made it a reality; thank you
Geania Kabolesha and Franziska Klauser!

FOREWORD

Many people have asked me why I wrote this book for women, and not for everybody. In my coaching practice, I have a particular passion for developing leadership in women. There are still only very few female role models in top positions in governments and organizations around the world. And often, the few highly successful female leaders have a very masculine style. I know from my own experience it is hard to find an effective leadership style without depending on masculine behaviors that we have seen work for others. As a woman, it is a great joy to find an authentic feminine leadership style. Having confidence is a critical element to be able to do that. I like to think this book will help many women have the courage to discover and unveil their fully authentic feminine leadership styles.

INTRODUCTION

From the shyest person in the world to the most arrogant person in the world, everyone can benefit from having more confidence. Our level of confidence broadcasts so much information about each of us in every moment of our lives, even if we are unaware that it does. When I say *confidence*, I mean believing in what you are doing, knowing that you are doing the best you can, and not doubting or second-guessing yourself. The goal of this book is to help each individual see her level of confidence clearly and learn some simple and effective exercises to help increase confidence in all areas of life.

A common issue that comes up in executive coaching sessions, especially with my female clients, is confidence. Even the most arrogant person can have a low level of self-confidence. At first glance, they seem like they know everything, but they actually have a lot of doubts, so they project false confidence as a kind of suit of armor. Then there are those of us who are genuinely low in confidence—and show it. These are the people to whom you do not dare point out errors or give feedback because you think it will genuinely hurt them. You may even fear that these people will break down in tears if you criticize them.

This book focuses on those of you who are somewhere in the middle. You feel confident much of the time, but certain situations or triggers cause you to suddenly feel paralyzed, at a loss for words, with a brain that suddenly doesn't seem to function properly.

Before you begin to read this book, rate your level of confidence on a scale of one to ten. A rating of one means: "I am very passive and rarely act on any of my thoughts. I only do new things when I am one hundred percent sure they will work out." A ten means: "I rarely second-guess myself. I am willing to do anything that springs to mind without worrying about the consequences." Take note of this number; we will come back to it later.

How confident are you?

My level of confidence is _____ out of ten.

Now take a few minutes to consider some questions about your current state of being. Grab a pen and paper or get on your computer and respond to these questions:

- Why did you give yourself that number?

- What is it like to have your current level of confidence?

- What is easy about having this level of confidence?

- What is difficult about having this level of confidence?

- What keeps you at this level?

As an executive coach, I could not start my book without a few coaching questions! Your answers will help you understand more about why you are at your current level of confidence. If you haven't already done so, I encourage you to take a few moments right now to write down the thoughts come to mind as you ponder these questions. No paper handy? I have provided a few blank pages at the back of this book for you to use. Your answers will stimulate valuable insights and prepare you for our journey together!

Margo C. McClimans

8

WHAT IS CONFIDENCE?

When I say confidence, I don't mean ego. I'm not talking about saying you are the greatest and putting yourself ahead of everybody else. Not at all; that is *egotism*. Egotism is the feeling or belief that you are better, more important, and more talented than other people.[1] True, deep-running confidence, on the other hand, is quiet. Quiet confidence is being aware of one's capabilities and strengths but not necessarily drawing attention to them.[2] If you believe in yourself,

---

1. (*Merriam-Webster Online*, n.d., "egotism")

then you will not feel the need to prove yourself to anybody. Therefore, you will go about your daily business believing in what you are doing, knowing that you are doing the best you can, and not doubting or second-guessing yourself. It gives you fuel to keep moving and keep doing the things that you need to do.

Another definition of confidence that I really like is, "Confidence is what turns thought into action."[3] People often have good ideas, but they don't take action because they don't believe in themselves or because they don't believe in their ideas. There is also a concept called "creative confidence."[4] Creativity is not about having more brilliant or better ideas than anybody else; it is actually about just being willing to

---

2. (Dolaman, Sim, and Wang 2010)
3. (Kay and Shipman 2014)
4. (Kelley and Kelley 2014)

say your ideas out loud, even if they are potentially wrong. This is the difference between creative people and "noncreative" people. It is not that creative people are smarter; it is just that they are more willing to share their ideas. They are more willing to be wrong, so they are more likely to keep coming up with new ideas and pushing their boundaries. Then, after a while, their umpteenth idea turns out to be the golden nugget.

If you don't have the confidence to speak up about your ideas, then you won't even start putting ideas on the table, and so you never get to the golden nugget. This is precisely the confidence I want to help you build. This is the willingness to put thoughts into action without constantly doubting yourself.

There are four different "channels" of confidence: breath, attitude, voice, and body. These four channels broadcast your level of confidence, whether you realize it or not. In other words, you can pick up on cues to determine whether someone is feeling confident or not by studying her breathing, attitude, voice, and body. We send signals via these four channels that transmit our level of confidence to the people around us. But it is not just about broadcasting confidence to the outside. It is about feeling confident on the inside, for your own sake. It is possible to "tune in" to these four channels to work on and raise your own genuine level of confidence from the inside. As you learn to adjust your frequency in these four channels, you will immediately feel an impact in your level of confidence. At first, it requires focus and attention, but the more you do the exercises I am about to explain, the more natural it becomes. Soon it will be second nature to feel confident in all four channels.

Margo C. McClimans

THE BREATH CHANNEL

We have all listened to presentations in which speakers seem breathless. They almost can't get the words out, and they sound like their mouths have gone dry. It is painful to witness because we know that horrible feeling ourselves! We have all been there at one point or another, whether we have made a presentation to clients or stood up before our colleagues in a meeting room. We hope the people listening don't notice, but we just cannot seem to multitask breathing and talking anymore!

Your breathing is a visible sign of your level of confidence. It is also a channel through which you can work to feel and exude more confidence.

Breathing is the most important channel of confidence because it supports the other three channels of confidence, as I will elaborate on in later chapters. Deep breathing reduces the levels of the stress hormone cortisol in your blood. To breathe properly, you need to hold your body in a strong, open position, which promotes confidence. I talk more about this in the chapter about body later in the book.

Our bodies produce cortisol when we are under stress. Cortisol impacts our physical well-being in many ways, most of them negative. When cortisol pumps through our veins, it is scientifically proven that we feel less confident.[5] One way to get rid of cortisol from our bloodstreams is to take deep breaths.[6] In her book *Success Under Stress*, Shirley Melnick talks about a certain breath that you can take to reduce the amount of cortisol in your blood. She calls it the "rapid clearing breath"; it entails breathing in through your nose for three counts and breathing out through your mouth for six. The point is to exhale to get out old, stale carbon dioxide and then take in fresh air. You breathe in relatively deeply for three counts, and the exhalation is double as long to rid your body of stress. If you do this for three minutes and if you could test your blood before and after, you would see a lower amount of cortisol in your blood. You will feel more confident.

We breathe all the time, so what is the big deal?

---

5. (Carney, Cuddy, and Yap 2010)
6. (Melnick 2013)

Many people breathe incorrectly and don't even know it. Breathing is one of the best resources we have because it is always available and it is free! Breathing properly helps us reduce stress levels, feel more relaxed, get our brain functioning at the highest possible level, digest food properly, and help our body restore its systems.

Typically, people breathe in a shallow manner from their chest; their chest rises only slightly when they breathe in and falls when they breathe out. That kind of breathing helps us survive, but if we want to *thrive*, we should be breathing deeply from our abdomens.

The lungs are like balloons; they do not actually have any muscles in them. Lungs expand and contract only because of the muscle underneath them called the diaphragm. The diaphragm moves up into the chest cavity like a plate being raised directly upward, pushing the air out of the lungs. At the end of the exhalation, the diaphragm automatically moves down into the abdomen to create more space for the lungs, which pulls in more air as you breathe in. If you breathe fully, letting the diaphragm go down into your abdomen as far as possible, your stomach will stick out a bit when you have a full, deep breath in your body. Therefore, if you are breathing fully, then you will feel your stomach move out, and your chest will not move much. Your chest and shoulders can be still, but your stomach should stick out when you have taken in a full, deep breath. As you exhale fully, your stomach goes in.

By the way, what have we women been taught to do with our stomachs? Hold them in, right? Especially on stage when everyone is watching us! No wonder it is so hard to feel calm and grounded when we are giving a speech or presenting in front of colleagues and clients. We can't breathe properly if we hold our bellies in all the time!

It is good practice to do some exaggerated breaths just to see how deep you can actually breathe and compare that to how you normally breathe.

Step 1: Inflate the "balloon." Start to inhale slowly through your nose, filling up your lungs and imagining that your stomach is a balloon you are inflating. Try putting your hand on your stomach so you can feel it beginning to protrude as you breathe in.

Step 2: Open the "auxiliary cavity." When you feel like the bottom part of your lungs is full (your balloon is fully inflated), then continue to inhale by slowly lifting your chest to create even more space for your lungs. Imagine a string attached to the center of your sternum being pulled directly up toward the ceiling until you cannot inhale anymore.

Step 3: Let the air out. Part your lips slightly, and control the speed of your exhale by keeping your mouth almost closed. Let the air escape through the small hole in your lips slowly and evenly. Feel your stomach deflate, and at the very end of the breath, you can even bend forward slightly to help let out the old, stale air.

In choir practice, we used to do breathing exercises like this to learn how to hold a note longer. On the exhalation, we would sing a note and see who could hold the note the longest. Timing yourself this way can be a fun method of practicing your deep-breathing ability. See how long you can make your exhalation. I have counted my own as long as thirty-six seconds, but I am sure many of you could make yours even longer!

It is incredible what a difference a few minutes of controlled breathing can make when it comes to increasing your confidence. First, learn how to breathe properly, and then practice this daily! Second, get over the fear of the momentary silence that will happen as you take a breath, which can be especially difficult when we are presenting. When we give a speech or presentation, for some reason, we have a completely distorted picture of how long silences are. We think that if silence lasts for more than a second or two, people will think we have forgotten something or somehow will find us unprepared. Au contraire! Silence is one of the best tools we have when making a presentation for three simple reasons.

1. Silence is an underappreciated attention-getter. Unfortunately, if we do not vary our voice enough, people stop listening; it becomes just sound to them. When we pause in our speech and allow a few seconds of silence, it creates a break in the sound and people look up to see what is happening.

2. People need time to ponder and respond. As a matter of practice, whenever I ask a question to my audience, I always allow seven seconds of silence for them to answer. Let me assure you, this feels like an absolute eternity when you are on stage. However, this is when people who are not normally the first ones to speak get a chance to chime in and contribute,

often bringing some of the most valuable insights to the group.

3. You get a chance to breathe! Once you get used to allowing and building in pauses and silence in your presentations, you can use those breaks as time to breathe properly. This gives you a chance to get your nerves under control, keep your cortisol levels to a minimum, and stay as confident as possible.

At the beginning of my career, I used to write on top of my presentation note cards in huge letters: SLOW...PAUSE...BREATHE! This reminded me to take a breath. It seems obvious, but sometimes we literally just *forget* to breathe properly! A little reminder can make all the difference.

THE ATTITUDE CHANNEL

Have you ever met a woman who just seems confident? She walks into a room and you just know she is not worried about what other people may think. It is not that she doesn't care what other people think; she is simply not *worried* about their opinions. Any group will contain some people who look confident and some people who do not look confident. You can just tell. The ones who have a confident attitude are the ones who seem to be reasonably comfortable around new people or circumstances. The key element of having a confident attitude is how you deal with your own saboteur.

Everyone in the world has a saboteur voice.[7] These are our inner critics. I believe that women suffer from them more than men and that the saboteur impacts women's choices more than men let it impact their choices. Of course, men are not immune! I have helped dozens of male managers learn to identify and pacify their saboteurs so they can achieve more.

In new or uncomfortable situations, a confident person just does *something* even if she doesn't know what she is supposed to do. A woman who has a confident attitude says, "I don't know what I'm supposed to be doing, but I'm not worried about getting it wrong. I am just going to speak to whomever I feel like about whatever I feel like." That

7. (Whitworth, Kimsey-House, and Sandahl 1998)

is what happens when we are able to let go of the saboteur voice. On the other side of the coin, the women who do not seem confident may not have a confident attitude. They are the ones who don't initiate things; they wait until someone speaks to them rather than walking up to people and reaching out to shake their hand. My experience is that they have a loud saboteur voice in their ear, telling them to hold back.

Saboteur comes from the French word *sabotage*, which is derived from the word *sabot*, a heavy wooden shoe worn by factory workers. In the early 20th century, unhappy workers would throw their sabots into the wooden gears of the textile looms to break the cogs because they feared that automated machines would render the human workers obsolete.[8] They sabotaged

---

8. (Hodson and Sullivan 1995, 69)

the machines with their sabots. Therefore, the workers' fears of change and their deep fears of becoming obsolete caused them to destroy the path to change. That is exactly what our inner saboteur does to us. Our saboteur wants to keep the status quo because whatever we are doing now has not killed us, so it must be safe. It stops us in our tracks whenever we want to step out, do something new, try something risky, grow, or develop a new behavior. A saboteur can be an incredibly strong force, provoking fear and anxiety in us that can be debilitating. Don't get me wrong; the saboteur is not evil. It is just our own ego trying to keep itself safe and free of any potential pain or embarrassment.

For example, imagine an office party at your new place of work. It happens to be your first day and you know no one. Instead of standing by yourself, you decide you want to go and speak to someone. Your saboteur tells you, "Those people don't want to talk to you," or "They are perfectly happy talking there, and you would be a disruption," or "You would seem overly eager if you introduce yourself; you would look silly," or "That person hasn't noticed you, so there's no point in saying hello." Sound familiar? Every woman's saboteur says something slightly different to her, yet the theme is often the same: "You are not good enough." Everyone has this voice, from the most confident to the meekest; it is just that not everyone *listens* to it all the time.

So, in the new workplace scenario, a person who has a confident attitude will brush aside the saboteur's commentary, confidently walk up to a new group, and make eye contact with the person speaking. A person who does not have a confident attitude, however, will heed the saboteur's warnings (usually without even realizing there was a saboteur at all) and stay glued to the spot, maybe pulling out her cell phone and having a look. A big difference between these two people is their ability to be in the here and now. The saboteur constantly pulls you out of the present moment to focus you on past failings or anxiety about future consequences. Like the Wizard of Oz's Wicked Witch of the West who melts away when she gets wet, your saboteur voice melts away as you bring your focus back to the present moment.

This is where the low-hanging fruit lies for those of us who find ourselves somewhere in between those two attitudes. The power comes in sharpening our skill of *noticing*. First, we have to notice that the saboteur is talking, bring ourselves back to the present and then we can choose to either ignore it or consciously say to ourselves, "It's OK. I'm going to try it anyway." That's the difference that allows people to start developing a confident attitude.

The strength of your confident attitude depends on how aware you are of your saboteur. Part of building self-awareness is also building awareness of the saboteur. Often, the saboteur builds on things that we've heard in childhood—critiques from parents and teachers or teasing from classmates and siblings. The things we hear about ourselves growing up help define how we perceive ourselves. Our saboteur voice picks up on the negative memories and uses them as potent fuel to prevent us from doing new things to keep us feeling safe.

My personal saboteur voice tells me many things, including, "You should be a good girl. Don't say something or do something that will make people not like you. You need to be accepted to survive." Even though nowadays I am much better at noticing and pushing aside my saboteur voice, when I am not aware of it, I am generally driven to always be nice, even if someone makes me angry. It tells me that I am not good enough or don't deserve what I want, so I should not speak up or ask for it. (This is usually bundled with feelings of guilt for not being grateful for what I have!)

Saboteurs like to remind us just before critical moments: "OK, don't forget, you better not do something that makes you look stupid—better not to do anything at all." Or, "Don't raise your hand and speak up unless you are one hundred percent sure of what you are going to say." What the saboteur really means is: "I want to keep you safe; I want to keep your ego protected."

Another saboteur of mine likes to try to convince me that I'm fat, which is something I got teased about when I was a little girl. The saboteur rips me away from the here and now and blinds me to my fit healthy body to remind of the past. No matter how thin I manage to get, I need to be constantly vigilant to notice that saboteur voice and remind myself that my weight is actually just fine now. And, yes, just maybe, I am even attractive.

As a young woman, one of my saboteur's favorite times to speak up was when I was near an attractive man. It would repeat, "You're not skinny enough and you're not pretty enough to get that guy." It would say, "You better attract men by being smart and funny." Luckily, I had a choice as to whether or not I would listen to that voice because I was aware of it. I would acknowledge the voice, take a few deep breaths, push this critical voice away, and then make some steamy eye contact with the guy across the room. It was amazing how well that worked.

Once you have a confident attitude, it will be easy to recognize the saboteur and ignore it. Or, just say to yourself, "No, I don't care. It's not true. I know that's just an old fear of mine. I'm going to do what I desire to do anyway."

The inner saboteur also likes to appear around the time of a job interview. When you apply for a job, of course you look at the requirements and skills needed. It is very difficult for everybody to meet 100 percent of those requirements. Internal research by Hewlett-Packard found that women apply only for jobs for which they feel they are a 100 percent match; men, however, apply even when they meet no more than 60 percent of the requirements.[9] In that case, a woman who doesn't apply may have a saboteur voice saying things like, "You're not good enough. They are not going to want you. You don't have enough experience. You haven't studied enough." Those are just assumptions on the woman's behalf that keep her "safe" from the potential difficulties she might face if she applies. The saboteur simply does not want change even though that might be a new and exciting job for the woman. It is a new step, and it's outside her comfort zone; therefore, the saboteur holds her back. The man who meets only 60 percent of requirements and applies anyway apparently does not hear the saboteur, or he is able to ignore it. Therefore, he is able to say, "Well, I meet most of the requirements. It's worth a try; let's just go for it." This is confidence; he is doing something even if he has

9. ("The Feminist Mystique" 2013)

doubt.

We will probably never get rid of the saboteur voices entirely. However, we can become very good at recognizing them. That ability gives us power because we then have a choice. If we are able to distinguish our saboteur voices from our true desires, then we will discover the magic antidote. The moment we recognize the saboteur, we can bring ourselves back to the present moment and say, "OK, my saboteur tells me I am not good enough. Is that true or is that something I want to ignore?" And then we have a choice—the power to turn thoughts into actions. The second we feel like we don't have a choice, we feel like victims. When we are in "victim mode," we are completely powerless.

My recommendation is not to try to eliminate or kill your saboteur, but instead, learn how to notice it. Get to know it like a lifelong companion so that you can have the choice at all times whether or not to follow it. Everybody's saboteur voices say something different to them, and you may have more than one.

Another example of how my good-girl saboteur comes into play is by telling me, "You are going to create an inconvenience for other people." An example would be this morning in the car. I was driving home from the tennis courts and came to an intersection that has no markings. In Switzerland, that means that whoever is on the right has the right of way. I had the right of way, but I saw this giant courier van pulling up fast, so I stopped and he abruptly halted. I proceeded, and he turned onto the same road behind me. This also happened to be a thirty-kilometer-per-hour (twenty miles per hour) zone. I assumed that because he was a deliveryman, he must know these roads well and must be in a hurry, and he probably wanted to zip around me so he could do his job. I noticed myself checking to see if he was following me closely because I felt I didn't want to get in his way since he was in a hurry.

Automatically my saboteur told me, "That guy is more important than me; I should be a 'good girl' and let him go around me." Then I thought, "No." I took note of my saboteur and said to myself, "No, I am actually going to drive the speed limit because that's what I am comfortable with, and if he is impatient, that is his problem." If I had not acknowledged my saboteur and instead let it take over, I might have gone faster than the speed limit just to make life easier for the deliveryman, assuming he wanted to go fast. The consequences might have been that I would drive dangerously or get a speeding ticket. See how the saboteur is actually self-sabotage? The saboteur thought that it was keeping me safe by making me look like a good little girl in the eyes of the courier man so he wouldn't be annoyed with me, but in reality, listening to that voice would have been a disservice to myself.

Another of my saboteurs tells me, "I'm not experienced enough." My whole life, I always found myself with older people—older friends, older classmates, older colleagues. This came to pass again when I first started working as a coach. I got a job with a large multinational corporation for the first time. Up until then, I had been doing coaching and leadership development with MBA students. Then I was selected to do some work for a large, well-known global organization. My first program consisted of three fellow coaches, twenty-four participants, and myself. The participants were managers for this organization who were coming from all over the world.

My saboteur was having a heyday because I was the youngest of my colleagues by at least ten years. If I had been looking at it from a neutral standpoint, I would have seen a group of four coaches that had a nice variety: men and women, different ages, different nationalities. But no, my saboteur wanted to emphasize that I was too young and therefore I didn't deserve to be there. It was my first time ever doing that kind of program. Part of the work entailed presenting concepts to and running exercises with all twenty-four participants. In addition, my fellow (highly experienced!) coaches were of course there listening as well.

It was my turn in front of the room. It was a simple

task; I had to run an introduction round. It was a one-minute challenge, so part of my job was to make sure people stayed within the minute, and I had to cut them off if they went longer. I went through the twenty-four participants without any issues. But then I got to my colleagues. One colleague went over the minute, and I jumped in and said, "Actually, that is over a minute." I kind of made a joke about it, but I did stop him, so he wrapped it up and didn't say anything else at the time. Immediately afterwards, while moving out into the hallway to go to the next session, he came up to me and said my reaction was not OK. After I asked what was not OK for him, he replied, "You have to let me talk more because I am one of the coaches" and added something about his credibility being impacted.

At this point, my saboteur was totally fueled, saying to

me, "See, you don't have enough experience. You should have known that." As if I should magically know things! Even though it was a small mistake, in the next session, I felt so much worse about myself, and I started doubting every little choice that I had to make. It was difficult to stay present. That is exactly the plague of the saboteur. If we are not aware of it, it knocks down our confidence levels even more. Consequently, I was even more nervous when I presented the next time. Luckily, I was able to use the technique of a mantra.

A mantra is a statement that people repeat frequently. People originally started using mantras as part of meditation to aid in concentration.[10] I could feel that I was nervous, and I combated that nervousness by building and then maintaining a more confident

10. (*Merriam-Webster Online*, n.d., "mantra")

attitude. I said to myself, "All right, I may not have as much experience as my colleagues, but I am a certified coach, and I have received lots of positive feedback about my coaching." I found a small but secure source of genuine confidence. I latched onto that area of confidence and held on even when I felt less confident about other areas.

I had been working with a coach myself over the previous year, and he had helped me discover a way of getting my energy back and feeling grounded. We had identified a very short exercise to do this. I just had to go somewhere I could see the sky and take a few deep breaths. So I went over to the window, took a few deep breaths (which always recharges me), and said to myself, "You know what? Even though I may be the youngest here, who knows? I may be the best coach they have." There was no way I could prove that sentence; however, there was a small chance that it might be true. Just that little but real possibility was enough to make me feel better. It had nothing to do with comparing myself to the other coaches. It wouldn't have mattered which other coaches were present; I had a mantra that helped me. My mantra was something for me to hang on to. All of a sudden, I could feel I was more confident. I was more comfortable if I made a mistake or if I stepped on somebody's toes here and there because I felt that chance that I may have been the best coach they had. My little mantra "I may be the best coach they have" was the perfect antidote for my "you're not experienced enough" saboteur.

How do you know if your saboteur voice is speaking?

A couple of signs show clearly that the saboteur is around.

1. You feel guilty. Take the example of the courier driver; I felt guilty for driving in front of him and slowing him down. That was the saboteur.

2. You say "I should" (instead of "I need to" or "I want to"). If you *really* think that you need to do something, you will say, "I need to get out of his way" or "I want to get out of his way," not "I should get out of his way." "Need" and "want" are completely different than "should." "Should" shows that you are doubting yourself rather than believing in yourself and being confident.

3. You are thinking about past mistakes or worried about future consequences. The saboteur pokes a hole in your confidence by taunting you with negative possibilities.

What tools do you need to live a fulfilling life and become more confident without letting the saboteur make your decisions for you?

Tools for Pacifying the Saboteur Voice

1. **Breathing** is the most important first step in gaining control over your saboteur. Breathing is so important that it has its own section in this book, and it also happens to be a handy antisaboteur tool. Breathing helps you distinguish the saboteur and access your confidence again. If you suspect that your saboteur is talking, stop whatever you are doing and take a few deep breaths from your stomach (as discussed in the section on breathing). Then notice, do you hear any old, familiar, saboteur-type voices? What does

your gut tell you? What does your heart tell you? Ask yourself, "What do I really want?"

2. **Replace "should" with "could".** If you find yourself using should in a sentence, practice replacing it with could. "I should really call her." becomes "I could call her". Suddenly, you have a choice! You *could* call her. Choice is empowering, and that brings a feeling of confidence.

3. **Mindfulness.** Your saboteur thrives on memories and predictions. Confidence requires courage, and courage requires focus and presence. The more you are able to gently guide your mind to focus on the present moment, the faster your saboteur voice will fade away.[11]

---

[11] The topic of mindfulness is very large and deserves further study. Andy Puddicombe explains it well in his TED talk "All It Takes Is 10 Mindful Minutes".

4. **End-of-day audit.** When you are first learning to recognize your saboteur, this exercise is especially helpful. At the end of your day when you are lying down to sleep, do an audit of your day. Think through your whole day and recall how many times your saboteur voice impacted your decisions or your behaviors. Do this every night for a week. You will probably be able to start drawing a pattern and understanding any recurring themes. This exercise is easier than trying to notice your saboteur in real time, and it builds your ability to catch your saboteur in action in the future.

5. **Building self-awareness.** The key to building confidence is to learn about yourself.

---

https://www.ted.com/talks/andy_puddicombe_all_it_takes_is_10_mindful_minutes

This way, you can be prepared to respond to challenging situations rationally rather than giving in to a saboteur-fueled, knee-jerk reaction. Take a few moments and answer the below questions about yourself. Once you have done so, you can use some of the confidence channels from this book to build up your confidence levels before or in those difficult moments.

a. What kinds of people or situations trigger a dip in self-confidence in you?

b. What is your "Achilles' heel?"[12]

c. What does your saboteur say, and when? Fill in the blanks:

    i. "You are too…"

    ii. "You are not…enough."

---

12. An Achilles' heel is a fault or weakness that causes or could cause someone or something to fail (*Merriam-Webster Online*, n.d., "Achilles' heel").

iii.   "I am always…"

iv.   "I never…"

Experiment with these the tools of breathing and mindfulness and the exercises of end-of-day audit and building self-awareness. Find out which one(s) feel good to you and have the best results. What I have noticed is that at first they can be somewhat difficult, yet it soon becomes second nature to use them. It requires focus and energy in the beginning, so hang in there!

What if my saboteur is right?

I talk about this topic a lot with my clients, and sometimes they are skeptical. They say things like, "Well, my saboteur is right! I have to listen to it; it's not just crazy talk. That stuff is true!" Some of what our saboteurs say to us is based on truth, and that's part of the reason why what it says is so attractive! It's so believable because it picks on your real fears, many of which are based on past experiences. The question is: If you follow what the saboteur says, will that prevent you from living up to your full potential? Probably!

Whether or not things actually went badly last time you were in similar circumstances, will you be living more fully if you go for it? Or will you be living more fully if you listen to your saboteur? I think the answer is clear. Even if you are convinced that your saboteur tells you the truth sometimes, you always have a choice whether or not you want to listen to it. And even if you still "obey" your saboteur voice 90 percent of the time, at least you can start making a change in your life and building more confidence. You will be amazed at what a difference this will make in your confidence levels over the long run.

THE VOICE CHANNEL

Another channel for confidence is the voice, including its volume, pitch, and speed. Our voices say a lot about how confident we feel. A confident voice is strong, clear, easy to understand, and just the right volume. We show our confidence by the way our voices sound, and we can feel more confident if we hear ourselves speaking more confidently.

I was running a leadership development program recently in which singer and renowned vocal coach Monika Ballwein was a guest speaker. She spoke to a group of managers, most of whom had never had voice coaching, and helped some incredibly soft-spoken, reserved people sound confident and outgoing. The first thing she said was, "Your voice can be like a Ferrari, but most people drive theirs like a Fiat."[13] She meant that we use a very limited range of volume, pitch, and style in our voices. Our voices are often an underutilized resource.

Imagine your voice is like a piano keyboard; it has eighty-eight keys, but most of us only use ten to twenty of those keys. Many people believe that if they vary their voices too much, they will sound funny. I have worked with many people who receive feedback from me or others that they are too monotone. Some of them try to vary their voices, but their attempts are so small that they hardly make a difference. So I ask

---

13. (Ballwein.com 2014)

them, "What makes it difficult to start varying your voice and trying out some of these techniques?"

They say, "I feel like I am varying it a lot already," or "If I do any more, I'm afraid I'm going to sound stupid," or "I'm going to sound fake or like a clown." However, they can't hear themselves like others can. This phenomenon is very common.

Most people don't realize the impact that their voices can have because they have never experimented with the different things their voices can do. Think about voices that you've heard in your life, on TV, in person, or on video clips. What do unconfident voices sound like? They usually are very low in volume and the words are often mumbled. Now think about the people who are confident. There is something about volume; it is louder than less confident people, but not necessarily overly loud.

Somehow, those voices are easier to understand. The volume is just right to be able to hear them without feeling like they are yelling. They don't feel they have any reason to hide what they are saying. When people feel confident about what they have to say, they make sure that others can hear them.

Think about yourself in any recent group discussion. When you feel like you have the right answer, you speak in a way that you know people will hear you. However, if you're not sure of yourself, you may say things in a lower voice. That way, if they hear and it's correct, then you have nothing to worry about; but if they don't hear it and it was the wrong answer, then you won't risk feeling embarrassed. Somehow, this feels safer. However, it is also potentially self-sabotaging to your confidence because if people do not hear your contribution, then someone else may bring up the same idea and receive all the credit. Or worse, your saboteur may convince you that people heard you and purposefully ignored you or shunned your idea.

The most confident women are comfortable being heard, being wrong, and being willing to be corrected and learn. They would rather make a mistake than to share ideas in a half-hearted manner. Again, confidence is not just about speaking louder. Sometimes the least confident people are overly loud because they are uncomfortable.

A confident voice is also the right pitch—usually lower rather than higher. Sometimes when we're nervous, we tense up, and part of this tension is held in our throat, which means we will likely start talking at a higher-than-natural pitch. Probably right now, as you read this book, you can feel that the muscles in your throat are relaxed. The level of tension in our muscles is what makes the difference between that nervous high-pitched voice and a more relaxed voice.

If you feel nervous or insecure, take a moment to pay attention to your neck and throat muscles. Take a deep breath and relax them as much as possible. It is very simple if you are conscious of it.

The speed of your voice is also an area to keep an eye on. Most of us speak much more quickly than we realize. The hardest part is realizing that we are speaking too quickly in the first place. The best way to learn if you are speaking too quickly is to ask for feedback from others. That's a universal rule for personal development: Get feedback so you can improve. Practice alone does not make perfect; we also need to learn how others perceive us from the outside. Another helpful exercise is to practice exaggerating how slowly you speak. It may feel funny to do this, but it is helpful to practice the range of speed you are capable of.

You can detect when people are not confident not only by low volume, high pitch, and high speed, but also by whether or not their voices tremor. When people are nervous, their voices may shake. I know it's happened to me many times, my voice shaking slightly during a job interview or on my first few client calls. However, this is also something we can remedy. This is where the fundamental tool of breathing comes in again. To raise the volume and steadiness of your voice, you need to have breath behind it. Picture the lungs like a bagpipe. The bagpipe has to have enough air in it to make a noise. When your lungs are empty and you attempt to say something loud, it's quite difficult, and your voice shakes. Now breathe in and with full lungs, say something loud. When you have full lungs, it is much easier to speak loudly, with no tremors. Your breath and your voice work in combination. To have a strong voice, you need to breathe properly, and to breathe properly, you need to be sitting up straight so your diaphragm isn't constricted. And surprise, surprise, when you sit up straight, you will look and start to feel more confident! All these elements are connected!

Vocal coach Monika Ballwein also talked about four different vocal modes that help to expand the range of one's voice:

1. Neutral: A soft-speaking voice without any particular adjustment to it. You can use it with or without air. (Breathing out slightly while speaking or not). Low volume.

2. Curbing: A suffering, whiny voice. For example, when a child wants something. Medium volume and somewhat metallic.

3. Overdrive: The voice you use at a football game when you want to yell, *"Go, team!"*. Loud volume and very metallic.

4. Edge: A voice with a lot of "metal" in it, using a lot of twang. Almost like a duck quacking. This voice is very useful in a crowded place. You have probably used it without realizing in a noisy restaurant when you needed to get the waiter's attention.

For all of these modes, you need to support your voice by breathing adequately. Practicing all four of those modes will help you learn control over your voice. If you're leading a group of people or you're in a crowd and need to get people's attention, you need to be able to use overdrive and edge. That's something most people have never purposefully experimented with. If you are unable or unwilling to use different modes, then you will have difficulty getting people's attention when you need to. It's important to be able to have this range so you can speak very softly when required and crank up your voice to megaphone strength when you need to.

Monika also talked about the color of sound. You can speak with "dark" sound color when you make more space in your mouth so it sounds dark and airy. You can produce a light voice when your mouth and throat have less space. Compare it with a clap; more space between your hands means darker sound color, less space (clapping with flat hands) means lighter sounds color. Your voice is equipped with an incredible range. You can choose. It is not only black and white; a whole spectrum of color can help you vary how you communicate your message.

In summary, it's about experimenting, practicing, and finding ways that you haven't been using your voice until now. Next time you are in the shower, practice making your voice darker or lighter or practice seeing the difference when you tighten or relax your throat. Give yourself the opportunity to start playing on more keys of the keyboard.

The channel of voice reveals your confidence level, and it is one way that you can increase your impact. By using a greater range of voice, supported by proper breathing, you convey your point more effectively. Once you take the steps to breathe and support your voice properly, your self-assuredness will also get a boost, creating a virtuous cycle.

Margo C. McClimans

THE BODY CHANNEL

The body and the brain can work together to help us feel confident. We should do everything in our power to make it easier for ourselves to be confident. We unwittingly do many things that go against our own confidence simply in how we hold our bodies.

As mentioned in the chapter about breathing, certain hormones in the blood either create stress or create confidence. Research from Amy Cuddy and other scientists at Harvard and Columbia University has found that the levels of cortisol and testosterone in our blood impact our feelings of confidence. The adrenal gland produces the hormone cortisol in response to stress. It generates energy to prepare for exertion or dealing with threats. It generally makes us feel anxious—and hence, less confident. Testosterone, on the other hand, is a hormone that reflects and reinforces feelings of status and dominance. It generates feelings of confidence and risk tolerance.[14]

Men and women alike feel more confident when we have higher levels of testosterone coursing through our veins. Levels of testosterone in our blood rise in anticipation of a competition and also after a victory. The converse is true after a perceived defeat. We are more willing to take risks when the levels of testosterone in our blood are high. No wonder our

---

14. (Carney, Cuddy, and Yap 2010)

confidence goes down after losing, and no wonder we often find it hard to get back on the horse and try again!

When I first learned that increased testosterone helps contribute to confidence, I thought, "Great, I'm supposed to have testosterone? What does that mean—that I have to grow hair on my chest to feel confident?" Of course, I was associating testosterone with men. It is in fact the male sex hormone, and estrogen is the female sex hormone. However, both men and women have both estrogen and testosterone in their systems. Fortunately, increasing our level of confidence requires only a tiny boost of testosterone. Don't worry; we won't become manly if we boost the testosterone in our systems! The fact that the male sex hormone encourages feelings of confidence makes it no surprise that a so-called confidence gap exists between men and women. We're built that way! Yet, we have many healthy, simple, and fast ways to increase our body's sense of confidence.

We can impact the levels of cortisol and testosterone in our blood. In her TED talk[15], Amy Cuddy explains that the ways we hold our physical bodies actually send a message to our brains that tells our bodies to produce either cortisol or testosterone. High-power poses increase testosterone and lower cortisol, and low-power poses do the opposite.

High-power poses are those body positions that take up space—positions that make us feel strong. High-power poses include putting your feet up on the desk or leaning back with your hands crossed behind your head. Another one is standing like Wonder Woman with your legs straight, feet solidly on the ground, and

---

[15] (Cuddy 2014)

fists on your hips. Cuddy also refers to power poses in the animal kingdom, such as when peacocks spread their feathers or cobras open their hoods. These poses not only display dominance, but they actually create a feeling of dominance. This is true in humans too.

Cuddy also shares the phenomenon that when humans experience victory, they tend to raise both arms in the air in the shape of a V. Even people who were born without sight do this when they win something great. Even though they have never actually seen anyone pose that way, it is a natural response to that feeling of victory. Power posing is an instinctual part of our human makeup.

Conversely, we also have what Cuddy calls low-power poses. With these body positions, we are closed up or make ourselves small. For example, crossing our legs, crossing our arms, touching our neck, and folding up all manage to make us seem smaller. I can't help but notice that these low-power poses are very similar to the "ladylike" behavior women are encouraged to learn as adolescents (e.g., cross your legs when you sit, keep your hands folded, rest your hands on your lap). We are certainly not encouraged to drape an arm over the chair next to us or take up lots of space! I am not saying we should burn our bras and start sitting with our legs spread, but I do think it is important to recognize those moments when we need to bolster our confidence and check to make sure we aren't overly "folded up" physically in that moment.

When we hold our bodies in low-power positions, we tell our brains that we're not safe and that we need to protect ourselves. In turn, the body creates the stress hormone cortisol, which makes us feel under threat.

Cortisol is not an "evil" hormone. It has its time and its place. Together with adrenaline, it helps us respond to challenges and tells the body to prepare for threats. Cortisol triggers a higher heart rate, higher blood pressure, and more perspiration because it is telling the body, "You may need to protect yourself!" It has an important function, but when it remains elevated over time, it has been linked to stress-related illnesses[16] and of course lowered self-confidence. Elevated levels of cortisol in the blood are linked to a whole host of nasty complications such as increased chances of osteoporosis,[17] loss of collagen in the skin,[18] increased blood pressure,[19] negative impact on fertility,[20] and many others.

---

16. (Mayo Clinic Staff 2014)
17. (Knight, Kornfeld, Glaser, and Bondy 1955, 176–181)
18. (Kucharz 1987, 229–237)
19. (Kennedy 2014)
20. (Nelson 2011)

In short, we should make it top priority to keep our cortisol levels low! How? There are many ways besides just holding power poses and taking deep breaths. Many things are associated with reducing cortisol levels, including massage therapy,[21] music therapy,[22] laughing,[23] taking a walk,[24] and dancing.[25] No wonder we love those things! Who would have thought getting a massage might contribute to your confidence?

The key is to be aware about what messages we are sending to our brain by what we do with our body. There are so many simple shortcuts; it's incredible how little we use them. I know many people who watch Amy Cuddy's TED Talk but still don't take the

21. (Field, Hernandez-Reif, Diego, Schanberg, and Kuhn 2005, 1397–1413)
22. (Uedo et al. 2003, 451–453)
23. (Berk, Tan, and Berk 2008, 946)
24. (Starks, Starks, Kingsley, Purpura, and Jäger 2008, 11)
25. (Quiroga Murcia, Bongard, and Kreutz 2009, 14–21)

time to do what she recommends, such as hold a power pose for one minute in preparation for a stressful situation. It only takes one minute!

I was able to use these tips recently during a tennis tournament. I love tennis and being on the court, but sports have always been the area in my life where I feel least confident. I decided to challenge myself by entering a tournament this year. I was shocked at how difficult it was to keep my confidence out of the gutter. I underestimated the emotional impact of a formal competition. So I decided to stand in a Wonder Woman position every single chance I got. Between points, during breaks, and when changing sides, I would stand or walk with my fists on my hips (racket in one hand), take deep slow breaths from my stomach and focus on sounds I heard and sensations I felt at that moment in order to be present. The positive impact it had on my game was incredible!

You have so many simple tools on your side to support you in feeling confident. They are free and available any time, and you can use them by choice as many times as you want, whenever you want. You don't even have to draw attention to yourself if you don't want to. You don't necessarily have to stand up and put your arms in the air. You can take small steps. Notice what you are currently doing that may inhibit your level of confidence, and stop doing it! Open yourself up physically. Take up a little bit more space. Take a few deep breaths from your diaphragm. We can do these things anytime we want even if we're in a meeting.

When you start to get stressed, your body tells you so. Your heart rate starts to rise, and your palms start sweating. This is a gift, actually! A lot of us think, "I can't stand it when I start sweating and can feel my heart pounding. It distracts me. It's a real problem."

However, it is a *gift* if our heart rate rises. It's a signal to say, "OK, I need to pause a minute and make a shift." That shift could be as simple as sitting up straighter, uncrossing your legs, taking some deeper breaths, bringing your focus to the present moment, remembering your personal mantra, or noticing the saboteur voice. Do yourself a favor and make a shift. Even one small adjustment will make a difference. You can't control what other people say or do that may trigger a lack of confidence in you, but you can control your body, your mind, your voice and your breath. Remember, you are the *only* authority in your life! You have the power to access your confidence when you need it!

Margo C. McClimans

TAKING ACTION

Becoming more confident comes with learning what you transmit to the outside via your attitude, your voice, your breath, and your body and, if need be, making an adjustment to those channels to feel more confident from the inside.

At this point, you may be thinking, "OK, this is not rocket science!" That's right—this stuff is simple! However, beware: simple is not always easy. Don't forget to continually and regularly check your channels (breath, attitude, voice, and body). Are you doing everything possible to support yourself in all of them?

Remember the rating you gave yourself at the beginning of this book? In a moment, I am going to have you set a goal for yourself. Please don't expect to be at a ten just because you have finished this book. Learning about these tools is just one part of your journey. Now the real work begins!

Now for some more coaching questions to help you build an action plan for yourself:

- You rated yourself _____ at the beginning of this book. What small action would you have to take to raise your confidence level to the next highest number?

- What number would you like to achieve? (It won't be a ten for everybody.) _____

- What would it feel like for you to be at your goal level of confidence?

- What would be different in your life?

- How will you feel physically, emotionally and mentally different when you reach your goal confidence level?

Get familiar with your goal and how life will be once you reach it. Know exactly where you want to be and how you want to feel.

- Which channel could provide a quick win for you? (e.g., attitude, breath)

- What is the first shift you are going to make to feel more confident in that channel?

- What else?

Margo C. McClimans

MY ACTION PLAN

My goal is have a confidence level of _____.

To move in that direction, my first three actions are:

1. I am going to start by…

    _____.

2. I will also…

    _____.

3. And I will…

    _____.

Write down your goals and check back every few months to see how you are doing. To support yourself even more, share your goals with someone who can help hold you accountable by asking how it is going and giving you feedback.

I am going to ask _____ to support me in reaching my goals. I will speak to this person about this by (date)_____.

I hope you have enjoyed this book. I wish you, as the Italians say, *forza e corraggio* (strength and courage) for your journey!

Warmly, Margo

ABOUT THE AUTHOR

A certified executive coach and leadership development trainer, Margo C. McClimans, CPCC, owns the company Coaching Without Borders, an organization that collaborates with over two dozen coaches to serve global leaders in Europe, US and Asia.

McClimans graduated with a bachelor's degree in international relations before earning an MBA in international business. After working in the import/export business in the US and Italy, Margo was "discovered" as a coach in 2005.

Having worked with over two thousand managers of over sixty nationalities to develop their leadership skills, McClimans has spoken at multiple women's leadership conferences, been selected to run WIN Conference workshops, and guest lectured at various business schools in Europe.

McClimans has lived in six countries on three continents and currently lives in Zürich.

http://www.coachingwithoutborders.com

Twitter: coachwoborders

REFERENCES

Ballwein.com,. (2014). CVT Vocalcoach Monika Ballwein
- Start. Retrieved 24 July 2014, from
http://www.ballwein.com

Berk, L., Tan, S., & Berk, D. (2008). Cortisol and
Catecholamine stress hormone decrease is associated
with the behavior of perceptual anticipation of
mirthful laughter. *FASEB J*, *22*(1), 946.

Carney, D., Cuddy, A., & Yap, A. (2010). *Power Posing: Brief
Nonverbal Displays Affect Neuroendocrine Levels and Risk
Tolerance* (1st ed.). Psychological Science. Retrieved
from
http://www.people.hbs.edu/acuddy/in%20press,%2

0carney,%20cuddy,%20&%20yap,%20psych%20scie
nce.pdf

Clinic, M. (2014). Chronic stress puts your health at risk. *Mayoclinic.org*. Retrieved 24 July 2014, from http://www.mayoclinic.org/healthy-living/stress-management/in-depth/stress/art-20046037

Deutsch, E. (1978). [Pathogenesis of thrombocytopenia. 2. Distribution disorders, pseudo-thrombocytopenias]. *Fortschritte Der Medizin, 96*(14), 761--762.

Dolaman, W., Sim, L., & Wang, A. (2010). *Quiet Confidence* (1st ed.). Georgetown University. Retrieved from https://blogs.commons.georgetown.edu/aw366/files/Quiet-Confidence_Final.pdf

Field, T., Hernandez-Reif, M., Diego, M., Schanberg, S., & Kuhn, C. (2005). Cortisol Decreases And Serotonin And Dopamine Increase Following Massage Therapy. *Int J Neurosci, 115*(10), 1397-1413. doi:10.1080/00207450590956459

Hodson, R., & Sullivan, T. (1995). *The social organization of work* (1st ed., pp. Chapter 3 pg 69). Belmont: Wadsworth Pub. Co.

Kelley, T., & Kelley, D. (2014). Creative Confidence by Tom & David Kelley. *Creativeconfidence.com*. Retrieved 22 July 2014, from http://www.creativeconfidence.com/

Kennedy, R. (2014). Cortisol (Hydrocortisone). *The Doctors Medical Library*. Retrieved 22 July 2014, from http://www.medical-library.net/content/view/1401/41/

Knight JR, R., Kornfeld, D., Glaser, G., & Bondy, P. (1955). Effects of Intravenous Hydrocortisone On Electrolytes Of Serum And Urine In Man. *The Journal Of Clinical Endocrinology \ & Metabolism,15*(2), 176--181.

Kucharz, E. (1987). Hormonal control of collagen metabolism. Part II. *Endocrinologie*, *26*(4), 229--237.

Melnick, S. (2013). *Success under stress* (1st ed.). New York: Amacom.

Merriam-webster.com,. (2014). Achilles' heel - Definition and More from the Free Merriam-Webster Dictionary. Retrieved 25 July 2014, from http://www.merriam-webster.com/dictionary/achilles'%20heel

Merriam-webster.com,. (2014). Egotism - Definition and More from the Free Merriam-Webster Dictionary. Retrieved 25 July 2014, from http://www.merriam-webster.com/dictionary/egotism

Merriam-webster.com,. (n.d.). Mantra - Definition and More from the Free Merriam-Webster Dictionary. Retrieved 24 July 2014, from http://www.merriam-webster.com/dictionary/mantra

Nelson, R. (2011). *An introduction to behavioral endocrinology* (1st ed.). Sunderland, MA: Sinauer Associates.

Petty, R. (2014). The Confidence Gap. *The Atlantic*. Retrieved 18 July 2014, from http://www.theatlantic.com/features/archive/2014/04/the-confidence-gap/359815/

Quiroga Murcia, C., Bongard, S., & Kreutz, G. (2009). Emotional and Neurohumoral Responses to Dancing Tango Argentino: The Effects of Music and Partner. *Music And Medicine*, *1*(1), 14-21. doi:10.1177/1943862109335064

Soffer, L. (1961). *The Human Adrenal Gland* (1st ed.).
    Philadelphia,: Lea & Febiger.

Starks, M., Starks, S., Kingsley, M., Purpura, M., & Jäger,
    R. (2008). The effects of phosphatidylserine on
    endocrine response to moderate intensity exercise. *J
    Int Soc Sports Nutr*, *5*(1), 11. doi:10.1186/1550-2783-5-
    11

The Economist,. (2013). The feminist mystique. Retrieved
    23 July 2014, from
    http://www.economist.com/news/books-and-
    arts/21573524-what-must-change-women-make-it-
    top-feminist-mystique

Uedo, N., Ishikawa, H., Morimoto, K., Ishihara, R.,
    Narahara, H., & Akedo, I. et al. (2003). Reduction in
    salivary cortisol level by music therapy during
    colonoscopic examination. *Hepato-Gastroenterology*,
    51(56), 451--453.

Whitworth, L., Kimsey-House, H., & Sandahl, P. (1998).
    Co-active coaching (1st ed.). Palo Alto, Calif.: Davies-
    Black

YOUR NOTES

Margo C. McClimans

Margo C. McClimans

Margo C. McClimans

36035663R00064

Made in the USA
Lexington, KY
04 October 2014